DOMESTIC ABUSE AND DOMESTIC VIOLENCE HELP FOR ABUSED WOMEN AND DOMESTIC VIOLENCE SURVIVORS

OVERCOMING YOUR PAST ABUSIVE RELATIONSHIPS

TRANSFORMING YOUR PRESENT

EMBRACING YOUR FUTURE

LIVING THE LIFE YOU DESERVE

ROBERT MOMENT

LEGAL STATEMENT

ISBN 10 : 0-9799982-2-0

ISBN 13: 978-0-9799982-2-5

This publication is designed to provide accurate and authoritative information with regard to the subject matter covered. It is sold with the understanding that the publisher and author is not engaged in rendering psychological, counseling, legal, accounting, medical or other professional advice. If psychological,counseling, medical, legal advice or other expert assistance is required, the services of a competent professional person should me sought.

> From the Declaration of Principles jointly adopted by a Committee of the American Bar Association and a Committee of Publishers and Associations.

Contents

Introduction

Reclaiming Your Life Today

If you've ever experienced any form of domestic abuse or violence, you know how difficult it can be to overcome your past, transform your present, and embrace your future. Whether you've been physically, mentally, emotionally or sexually abused, you will bear the scars forever. However, learning to deal with those scars, accepting them, and moving on is the basis for offering you the opportunity to live the life you deserve.

In this book, written for women who have left an abusive relationship or situation. If you're still in an abusive relationship, we encourage you to seek immediate help, and if possible, find a local women's shelter for your safety.

In this book, we'll discuss a number of ways to live that life you deserve, utilizing what we call the **MIA Formula**, which stands for *motivation, information, and action*. Information and knowledge will give you power - really. The information in this book will give you the confidence, knowledge and power to – *Take Charge of You*.

Information has the capability to transform your life. Knowing that you're not alone also helps, although you wouldn't wish any type of abuse or violence on anyone else. Unfortunately, it happens, more often then we'd like to believe.

Reclaim your life, today. We strive to show you how you can release your anger, grief, and even hatred, to reclaim your emotions. We hope to guide you toward forgiveness, as forgiveness truly does set you free.

Believing in yourself is also extremely important as you begin your journey to self discovery. Self-discovery involves introspection and a serious consideration of how you think, as well as why you think the way you do.

We'll guide you on your journey toward healing, offering keys to emotional health and wellness. Most of all, our goal is to help you overcome your past, transform your present and embrace your future. You do this by not only understanding yourself, but by understanding the power of self-love and acceptance.

No book of this kind would be complete without offering a number of helpful resources and support systems that you can utilize in your community to help you along. After any disappointing or even devastating relationship, it's often difficult to differentiate between a healthy and not-so-healthy relationship. We'll touch upon that subject and also address how you can overcome your fear of loving again.

Finally, we'll talk about daily affirmations that will help you be happy again.

So, we're not saying your journey will be easy, or that this book will provide an answer to all your uncertainties and questions. You've started on one of the most difficult journeys you've ever taken, but it's an important one. Whether you're involved in an abusive relationship at the moment or have left one behind, it's important to reclaim yourself.

Live for yourself, love for yourself, and do everything you can to make those scars fade. They won't go away completely, but you can relegate them to the past while at the same time looking toward the future.

The basic tenets we'll touch upon in this book to overcome your past, transform your present and embrace your future will include:

- Showing you how to forgive – we're not only talking about forgiving an abuser, but forgiving yourself. Many women feel guilty and ashamed for staying in abusive relationships. In order to completely heal and transform your life, it's important not to carry hatred in your heart. Forgiveness *will* truly set you free.

- Encouraging you to believe in yourself - you *are* worth every effort. You *are* unique, special and deserving of happiness, safety, and security. After you've been knocked down, it's not always easy to get back on your feet, but you can do it.

- Teaching you how to heal - emotional and mental
  healing is just as important as physical healing.
  We'll guide you along your way toward learning
  how to take steps to heal emotionally, mentally, and
  physically.

- Providing tips on how to overcome your past - this
  is often the most difficult part for many abused
  individuals, but is an important step in embracing
  your future and living the life you deserve.

- Offering ways to transform your present - whether
  that means an attitude adjustment, surrounding
  yourself with loved ones, or finding support, it *is*
  possible to transform your present in order to
  overcome your past and embrace your future.

- Guiding you toward embracing your future and
  living the life you deserve. - you *can* overcome.
  Using helpful resources and support systems that
  we'll offer in this book, you can learn to live and
  love again.

Throughout this book, we'll utilize the **MIA Formula** in
order to help you along on your journey. The most
important thing to know before we get started is that you
are **loved**. You are special, just for being who you are. It
doesn't matter where you come from, how much money
you make, or if you have a job or not. You are worthwhile.

7

The first step in overcoming domestic abuse and violence of any kind is to reclaim your emotions. We'll talk about that next.

Chapter 1

Releasing Your Anger and Reclaiming Your Emotions

No doubt about it, getting rid of pent-up anger and resentment is tough. It can be especially tough for anyone who's experienced domestic violence or abuse, regardless of what type.

However, by understanding the detrimental effects of anger, not only on your emotions and mental state, but also on your body, may encourage you to find ways to let it go. According to recent medical research, high levels of anger and stress have a very detrimental effect on heart health, and can even increase one's risk of heart disease.

In case you're wondering how anger actually contributes to heart disease, it all goes back to the physiological effect on the body's arteries and the heart muscle itself. High emotion, including anger, is believed to activate certain stress hormones caused by one's "fight or flight response". Those hormones that gush through the body include cortisol and adrenaline, each of which increases heart rate. Anger and high emotion also increases one's blood pressure, which is caused by constricting blood vessels. This constant pressure on the arteries is not good for the heart either.

High emotion increases creates high levels of adrenaline and cortisol, which stream through the body. After time, this can have a toxic effect on the cardiac system. Basically, it causes wear and tear and can speed up atherosclerosis, a medical term that defines the accumulation of fatty plaque or clogging in the arteries. Because the heart has to pump harder to get the blood through those vessels, not only your heart is affected, but you also experience higher levels of glucose and fat globules in those blood vessels, leading to damage to the arteries, not only of the heart, but others in your body.

Chances are that if you experience high levels of stress and anger, you may also be dealing with depression and negative emotions. The Journal of the American College of Cardiology performed nearly 50 studies in the last few years, which supported evidentiary findings between emotions and heart disease. Hostility and anger have been shown to definitely increase one's risk of cardiovascular issues. In fact, chronic stress and heightened emotions like anger can increase your risk to develop heart disease by nearly 20%.

Shall we talk about the detrimental effects of stress on the body? Emotionally, stress can cause a number of issues regarding your mood, including but not limited to:

- Lack of motivation
- Irritability
- Depression

10

- Anxiety

Physically, stress contributes to:

- Headaches
- Fatigue
- Upset stomach
- Sleeping problems

Emotionally and mentally, stress leads to a number of behaviors, including over-eating or under-eating. Many of us have succumbed to what we call "comfort eating" to deal with stressful situations, our emotions, and our anger and frustration with our environment. Others stop eating altogether, and risk conditions such as anorexia nervosa.

Long-term stress, hostility and anger in our lives also lead to increased risk of alcohol or drug abuse. Another behavioral aspect of anger and stress is social withdrawal. Many of us don't want to bother our loved ones with our emotions, or we feel uncomfortable about expressing them in front of others. Other times, you may get the impression that no one wants to hear about your feelings. Either way, you feel isolated and alone. This is also extremely stressful.

We've all heard of the best ways to manage stress, but physical activity, relaxation or meditation techniques, or engaging in practices like yoga or tai chi don't always help us overcome that stress. The important thing is to recognize the signs and symptoms of stress, as well as regularly assessing your emotional state during and after less-than-ideal domestic situations.

So, how do you get rid of your anger? How do you get a handle on your emotions and reclaim them as your own? Let's talk about that.

Getting Rid of Anger

Anger has a way of rooting itself deeply into our psyche. Resentment and anger often go hand in hand. At times, your feelings of anger and resentment can cripple your ability to get through the day.

We're not suggesting that you bottle up your anger or try to stamp it down and pretend it doesn't exist. It obviously does. However, it's important to deal with it and get rid of it in a positive and effective manner. Suppressing your anger or negative emotions only causes them to grow larger. For some, suppressing such negativity and anger for years can come back to haunt you later in life, or even hover over your head for years.

However, when getting rid of anger, resist the urge to yell or scream. This type of emotional response only increases the tension you may already be feeling and ultimately, doesn't resolve anything except perhaps to give you a sore throat.

People get rid of anger in different ways. Some people talk to a close friend, family member or religious figure in their community. Others literally "walk it off" by removing themselves from an environment that provokes angry or resentful thoughts. Still others write down their emotions and feelings in a journal.

MIA

When taking steps to reduce angry feelings, it's important to get down to the bottom of exactly why you're angry. This is not abroad consideration, but should give you the opportunity to focus on something specific. Why, exactly, are you angry? Do your best to identify whether you're angry about something that just happened, or if that anger is caused by something residual in the past.

Try to think of something that will lighten your mood. This can be incredibly difficult, but looking for the humor in situations can help make life seem more manageable.

Don't be embarrassed by your anger. We're human, and anger is a natural emotion. Accept your anger, but at the same time realize that sometimes, we don't have the power to control everything in our lives.

Once you've recognized and accepted your anger, think about how you can learn from it. Every difficult experience or situation in our life teaches us something. Perhaps your anger has made you stronger, or has encouraged you to be more independent. That's a good thing. Think of other ways in which your anger has propelled you to improve, physically, mentally, and emotionally.

Finally, recognize that the past is the past and nothing you do can undo that past. While you can be grateful that the past is over, try not to dwell on all the negative aspects of that past. Look forward. It might've been horrible, but you survived. You're strong, and have the capability to overcome your past and live the life you deserve.

Here's a final thought to getting rid of your anger. Pay attention to what you're thinking about when you're angry. If you find yourself dwelling on negative events, individuals or situations, force yourself to clear your head. Think more positive things, even if it's visualizing a mountain stream, rolling ocean waves, or the features of a loved one. Close your eyes and breathe slowly, focusing your attention on the here and now.

We'll conclude this section with a few tips on getting rid of anger for the long term:

- Appreciate the moment - shift your thoughts away from negative emotions and feelings.
- Smile - even if it's difficult.
- Think happy thoughts – we're not suggesting you minimize a traumatic event, but try to be grateful for the good in your life.
- Find stress release through sports, exercise, or a

hobby. Exercise releases endorphins, the body's own "feel-good" chemicals.

- If you're feeling especially down, avoid caffeinated products, alcohol and prescription or street drugs, which can only make you feel worse.
- Find a place where you can relax and calm down. After you've had a moment to relax, ask yourself why you were angry and how you can better deal with it the next time.
- Talk to close friends or family members or even a pastor.

It's not always the best thing to walk away from your anger, but to confront it, recognize it, and deal with it. Even if you have to resort to punching your pillow, do it to get rid of that burst of adrenaline and cortisol in your body. Then, if you're really angry, write down your feelings on paper. It doesn't matter what you do with the paper once you're finished, just let the emotion out. Don't hold it in.

Reclaiming Positive Emotions

It's easy to focus on the negative aspects in our lives. However, it's also extremely important to focus on the positive. When you focus on the negative over time, it's easy to forget what it feels like to feel secure and happy. When overcoming a violent or abusive domestic environment, you may feel that nothing is worthwhile anymore, that you or your opinions have no value. It's important to remember that you do, and realize that your opinions also matter.

Every day, no matter how down you're feeling, try to reflect on something positive. Think about something in the past, even yesterday, that made you happy inside, or provoked a smile. It doesn't matter whether that something is the site of a scampering puppy or the innocent smile you received from a child while walking by the schoolyard. Dig deeper into your memories and remember the times in your life that were happier, more carefree, and pleasant.

Rather than allowing those memories to depress you, recall them with appreciation and gratitude. Make a conscious effort to think of happy or pleasant things that have occurred recently. Doing so can subconsciously shift your thinking patterns from focusing on the negative to actually and actively seeking out the positive.

Think about an emotion that you haven't felt in a while. Whether that emotion is satisfaction, pleasure, acceptance, or even love, think of the types of emotions that you want to feel more often. By merely thinking of the positive emotions you want to experience, your mind is more apt to seek those emotions. Start spending several minutes a day by yourself just thinking about and remembering what such emotions felt like to you. Force those memories up inside you and revel in the positivity such emotions evoke.

For example, when you feel uncertain and need a burst of

courage or self-confidence, think of something successful that you've accomplished in life. When you're stressed out due to your daily routines or challenges, think of a memory or emotion that brought you serenity. Instead of focusing on the negative, look around you. Experience the sensation of joy or pleasure in the splendor that surrounds you. It doesn't matter if you live in the mountains or the desert, near a beach or a mountain lake, look outside. Life is so much bigger than ourselves. The sun will rise and the sun will set. Go outside and enjoy the sunset, reveling in its beautiful colors. What emotions does watching a sunset or sunrise evoke in you? Think about it.

Again, we're not suggesting that you ignore your painful feelings, nor ignore the negatives in your life. We need to recognize these things. However, the goal in reclaiming your emotions is to gain more power over them. All your feelings need to be recognized, not just the negative ones, and not just the positive ones. Rather, it's all of them. It's all of your emotions and feelings that make you who you are.

Chapter 2

Forgiveness Will Set You Free

Perhaps one of the most difficult things for humans to do is forgive. However, the power of forgiveness is not merely focused on those whom we forgive, but on ourselves. In this section, we'd like to talk a bit about the power of forgiveness, physically and psychologically, and how you can learn to overcome difficult challenges and embrace our future.

You may not believe it now, but the act of forgiving can bring greater peace to yourself and to your soul. Forgiveness equates with freedom, and encourages a sense of cleansing and peace within yourself. Letting go of anger, resentment, jealousy or any other human emotion is challenging. Sometimes, we have to try several times before we actually succeed. However, success is possible. Let us show you how.

Achieving the Power of Forgiveness – the MIA approach

First, even if you don't want to, visualize the person who treated you badly or abused you. In a matter of seconds, you're likely to be bombarded with a number of emotions, frustrations, grievances, and perhaps even stronger feelings such as hatred. In a few more seconds, try to shift your concentration onto how you *feel*. Has your heart rate accelerated? Are you breathing faster? Do you feel tense? If you answered yes to any of these questions, you will benefit from the power of forgiveness to release you, gradually, yet ultimately, from such negativity.

Next, relax your shoulders and focus on breathing through your belly. Take four or five deep breaths while you focus on how your body begins to feel. If you find it difficult to concentrate on your breathing after evoking the vision of the person who hurt you, focus again on moving your belly in and out. It doesn't matter whether you're lying down or sitting while doing this exercise. Focus on the rhythm of your breath, and if you have to, watch your belly expand and contract as you focus only on breathing.

Now that you're focused on your breathing, think about something that gives you pleasure. It can be a vision of a beautiful location such as a beach, a mountainside, or the desert. The image that comes to mind can be someone you love, a place you like to be, or anything pleasant. Many of us have what we call our "happy places" – that place may be a location such as Disneyland, or it may be sitting on the bank of a river, fishing or throwing rocks. Your happy place can be a memory as well. Regardless, bring something that you love, or a place that brings you tranquility, into your thoughts. Soak in this image, trying to evoke all your senses. Now, literally envision the pleasure, the smells, the feelings, and the vision of your happy place directly to your heart.

Keep breathing and immerse yourself in the pleasurable sensations and memories of your tranquil image. Then, once again imagine the person who has hurt you, but this time, keep in mind the good feelings that your "happy place" has brought you, as those feelings, emotions, and sensory images will help protect you against the negativity of the person who hurt you.

Finding Solace

What's the purpose of such an exercise? The exercise is not designed to immediately cure you of anger, hurt or resentment, but to help you break the pattern of negative or stressful reactions that you feel when you think of the person who has done something bad to you. The more you surround yourself with positive and pleasant energies and memories, the more you're able to anticipate – and negate - the power of the person who hurt you.

Don't expect to change overnight. Studies have shown that any new habit takes approximately 15 to 25 days to develop. It doesn't matter if that new habit is exercising or dieting, or conversely, an attempt to quit smoking, drinking, or biting your nails. Give yourself, your body, and your mind, time to change both physical, mental and emotional reactions.

A quote by Nelson Mandela personifies the detrimental effect that holding onto resentment and anger does to you. *"Resentment is like drinking poison and then hoping it will kill your enemies."*

Rather, strive to forgive. Forgiving is not the same as forgetting, or for desiring that someone be punished for doing horrible things. When people commit crimes, they do deserve to be punished, but sometimes, that punishment should be left to God. Do what you can to begin your journey toward healing, recuperation, and transformation. Most often, your mental, physical and emotional well-being will increase if you have the power, and the capacity, to forgive.

Forgiveness is Self-Liberating

Forgiveness is truly self-liberating, and can set you free, of not only the difficult and painful past, but helps propel you toward a life of fulfillment. Forgiveness gives you the power to arm yourself and empower yourself to begin transforming your life. You may not believe it right now, but forgiving someone is one of the most freeing experiences you can enjoy.

The very act of forgiveness emphasizes your own ability to control your future. You can transform your understanding and your concept of not only right and wrong, but guide yourself toward principles and ways of life that will only enhance your transformation and help you embrace your future. *Forgiveness personifies your ability to create positive energy that is unrestricted by anything or anyone, around you.*

You can say that the power of forgiveness is the ultimate sense of control an individual can have. Freedom to forgive is a personal choice. It takes strength and courage to forgive someone who has abused you. The choice and power to forgive is the ultimate expression of our free will. However, do keep in mind that the inability to let go of resentment, anger or refusal to forgive someone of a past wrong may have a long-term and detrimental effect on your overall health and well-being.

No doubt about it - some people are very bad, and it can be incredibly difficult to forgive someone who has wronged you, hurt you, and destroyed your sense of confidence and self-esteem. However, do try to realize that holding onto resentment and refusing to forgive someone merely ends up hurting yourself. Not only are you emotionally trapped by those feelings, but those feelings may also affect your physical health and wellness.

Not only do we encourage you to forgive the person who has wronged you, through the strength of your faith, love and compassion, but to forgive yourself. We're human. We make mistakes in judgment. It doesn't do you any good to live in the depths of regret. Learn from your mistakes, and learn from the mistakes of others. Try to benefit, in any small way, from your experiences.

You may feel, at this moment, that forgiveness is impossible. The pain you have experienced, emotionally, mentally or physically, is too great for you to forgive. However, at the same time, it's important for you to realize that you have the strength, the courage, and the power to overcome anything in life, with dedication and determination. Believing in yourself is the first step toward forgiveness that will ultimately set you free.

Conclusion

Yes, forgiving someone is one of the most difficult things you may ever do in life, but may be one of the most important things you do on your journey toward your future. You've been in pain, felt disappointed and upset, and have grieved. However, think of this. How long do you want to hold onto that negativity before you move forward? Holding onto anger and resentment slows you down, and can overcome your every thought, emotion, or decision in life.

Forgiveness enables you to let go of the past, and the anger and pain it has cost you. Forgiveness gives you the power- and the chance - to focus on the now, and to shrug off that cloak or burden and continue onward.

Forgiveness comes from the heart and the soul. Yes, it can be one of the hardest things you ever do, but the sensation of relief and utter freedom that you feel when you have truly forgiven someone, from the depths of your heart, is one of the most freeing emotions you will ever experience.

Chapter 3

Believing in Yourself

Believing in yourself isn't always easy to do, especially when you've just come out of a violent or abusive relationship. The trauma, lingering emotions, and feelings of inadequacy are just a few that often hobble women at such a time. Self-confidence, and self-esteem, and trust in one's own abilities are often damaged, and many of us feel that we can't even trust our own decisions.

Believing in yourself involves reestablishing your sense of self-esteem, self-confidence, and ability to make wise decisions. You're smart. You can think things through. In this section, we'd like to offer a few tips and suggestions to help you get back on track.

Tips to Get You Started – the MIA Approach

Believing in yourself requires a bit of thought and contemplation. First, try setting some short-term goals. This will help you establish a sense of control over your own decisions and actions. Setting small goals, whether it's to get through today, tomorrow, or next week, is a start.

Goals can be emotional or physical in nature. For example,

you can tell yourself, "My goal for today is to feel confident." Alternatively, "My goal for this week is to exercise every day and watch what I eat."

Short-term goals should be simplistic in nature, and determined by your current emotional and mental state. The key is to set goals. As you achieve each goal, your confidence will increase.

Be careful at this point in setting too-lofty goals, as failure to reach them may hamper your self-confidence and self-esteem. If you've gained weight as a result of a violent or abusive relationship, develop an exercise and eating plan that you can manage in small steps. Don't set a goal to lose 20 pounds in one month. Instead, aim for one or 2 pounds a week. Strive to eat better, and be healthier. This doesn't mean that you can't enjoy "comfort foods" but rather that you pay attention to what you're eating and how it makes you feel.

The same approach can be taken with your emotional and mental outlook. No one expects you to bounce back from an abusive or violent relationship overnight. For some, the journey can take weeks, months, or years. Accept that. Deal with the emotions one at a time rather than all at once.

Another way to help you start to believe in yourself is to consider your failures or shortcomings. Don't feel bad about making mistakes or backsliding, whether you're starting on a new eating plan, an exercise routine, or a job-hunting endeavor. Instead, consider why you have failed to meet a goal or why you feel disappointed or disillusioned with yourself. Ask yourself questions:

- Am I not assertive enough?
- Am I too pushy? (Some women who have left a violent or abusive relationship may overcompensate when it comes to control. Be aware of this. If you find yourself being confrontational, too aggressive, or too "angry" when dealing with other people, potential employers, or even your work or school peers, take a step back and reassess your attitude and your emotions)
- Are you afraid?

These are just a few of the questions you can ask yourself to help you determine some of the 'whys' in your life.

Believing in yourself takes time. Many of us seek positive feedback in order to emphasize our value and contributions to work or family environments or situations. However, be realistic when determining your success at emotional, mental and physical improvement. For example, would you attempt to run a marathon without training? Your body will not be conditioned to run a marathon. The same goes for your ability to learn to believe in yourself once again.

Just Do it

Look at where you were, where you are now, and then
envision where you want to be. This will help you
determine exactly what you need to do to get there. Have
you made progress in the last few days, the last few weeks,
or even the last few months? Believe us when we say that
every day, you will start to feel stronger and more self-
confident. As you gain this strength and confidence, you'll
once again learn to believe in yourself and to trust your
own emotions, decisions, and actions.

When overcoming a violent or abusive relationship, it's
easy to feel self-conscious or be extremely sensitive to
criticism. However, when put correctly, criticism is a
wonderful tool to help us improve. Of course, there will
always be those who put you down or criticize you to make
themselves feel better, but for the most part, critical advice
offered by a friend, a family member, or a work peer can
help you recognize and then make changes to improve
yourself.

When learning to believe in yourself again, it's important to
focus on others and not just yourself. One of the best ways
you can do this is to help someone else. Volunteer at a local
organization, or at your local school, community center, or
long-term care facility or a nursing home. There's always
someone that needs a helping hand, and who, better than
you, to understand the needs of such individuals? The
ability to help others creates and builds self-respect and

self-esteem, each of which is necessary in order to begin believing in yourself once again.

Also, even though it may have been a long time, remember the dreams, aspirations and goals you used to have. How do you feel about them now? Is it, something that you would be interested in pursuing? Don't give up on your dreams, no matter how far in the future they may seem. When you believe in yourself, you give your best. When you believe in yourself, you'll be more successful.

Things to Avoid

When learning how to believe in yourself once again, it's important not to compare yourself with anybody else. Be who *you* want to be. It's fine to emulate someone else, but you can never walk in their footsteps. Because of your past experiences, your outlook on life will naturally be different from someone who has not experienced what you have.

Allow yourself to grow, emotionally and mentally, with each new experience. Don't let fear, hesitance, or uncertainty hold you back, but be confident. Every day, make a conscious effort to reach the goals you have set for yourself.

No one can achieve your goals for you. Self-improvement comes from within. Don't let the negative or critical comments or snipes from others determine who you are.

You know who you are, and you know what you feel and why you feel it. No one can tell you how to feel.

If you get knocked down to your knees, simply take a deep breath, stand up, brush yourself off, and move forward. People never get anywhere from standing still. No matter how hard it is, it's important to keep putting one foot ahead of the other. After all, you never know what's just around the next bend in the road.

Believe in yourself! If you don't believe in yourself, no one else will. However, before you can believe in yourself, you have to get to know yourself. This takes time and reflection, as mentioned earlier. Know how you feel about things and know which methods of tackling life's challenges work best for you in a variety of scenarios.

Try to keep your thoughts healthy and positive, and rely on your faith, friendships, and family for support when you feel weak or uncertain.

Don't dwell so often on asking yourself, "What did I do wrong?" Instead, turn the tables and ask yourself what you've done right.

Think of all the things that you've accomplished in your life. Remember all the times that you helped someone, loved someone, or achieved that goal or gained a boost of confidence and happiness from an action you performed. While it is difficult for anyone overcoming a violent or abusive past to find joy in life, it's there, if you take the time to look.

We all have days where we berate ourselves for doing something that we shouldn't have, for being grumpy, wallowing in self-pity, or even being mean to someone else. It's human nature. However, do your best not to let one day turn into several days, weeks, or months.

It can be incredibly exhausting to feel "down" all the time. When you believe in yourself and engage your daily activities with positive thinking, self-confidence and assurance, you'll be amazed at how much better you'll start to feel in a relatively quick time.

Try doing something that you haven't done in a while. Try your best, even if you're uncertain of your success. Whether it's going for a job interview, getting outside, or socializing with others, try. Don't tell yourself that you can't do it before you tried. After all, any effort, even if it fails, is better than not trying at all.

We also might suggest a simple writing exercise. Create a list of all the things that you believe you can do. You might be amazed at how many things you really can accomplish. What are your skills, talents, or habits? You may not have done them in awhile, but you still can, if you give yourself a chance.

By trying, and recalling all the things you can do, you'll

open your mind to limitless possibilities. You can succeed. Avoid self-defeating thoughts, and recognize and accept the fact that some things in life may be difficult, and out of your comfort zone, but you can do them if you try. Sure, you may not succeed in every endeavor, and you may get knocked down once in a while, but the important thing is to try. As we've mentioned before, you'll never get anywhere by standing still.

Conclusion

Believing in yourself doesn't come easy to many of us, especially those who have come out of a violent or abusive relationship. The lack of self-confidence and self-esteem one may feel can be overwhelming. However, the first step toward transforming your life and embracing your future relies on your ability to assess your position in life right this minute. We already know what's happened in the past, but what do we want to happen in the future?

Remember that you must be the driving force for reaching your goals, whatever they may be. No one can stop you from realizing your dreams but you yourself. While many of us find ourselves taking different roads to achieve our dreams, and some of us may never actually realize them, we gain joy in the mere attempt. So, you may never live in that grand mansion on a private estate, but in striving to reach such a goal, you may find yourself living in a neighborhood you never dreamed possible, or enjoying a job that offers you security that you never imagined.

Many of us will never realize our dream of going to the moon, but should that stop us from looking into the starry sky at night and imagining? It's also important to realize that even though such a dream may not be realized, it doesn't mean that you're a failure or that you haven't worked hard enough to achieve it - it doesn't mean that we can't believe, dream, and achieve.

Chapter 4

Your Journey to Self-Discovery

In this section, we'll briefly discuss what to expect as you make your journey toward self-discovery. What does self-discovery mean? It means envisioning possibilities, finding your positive, and the reasons for "because" that you make decisions and do things. Self- discovery is often a hard topic to define, because it means something different to nearly everyone.

According to the dictionary, self-discovery defines the process or act of achieving knowledge or understanding of oneself. It means understanding why you think the way you do, act the way you do, or why you make decisions the way you do. Self-discovery doesn't happen overnight, but evolves slowly, over time. It's the ability to seek the greatest potential in yourself.

For this reason, your journey to self-discovery may also include ways to improve and develop not only your capabilities, your self-esteem, and your confidence, but your greater understanding of your place in the world around you.

What Does Self-Discovery Involve?

Your journey of self-discovery involves a number of aspects including:

- Habits
- Emotions
- Beliefs
- Thoughts
- Expression
- Attitude
- Actions

Many of us develop habits in life, some good, some bad. Overcoming an abusive or violent relationship may require you to change some habits, some of which been ingrained for years. Overcoming wariness, suspicion, and doubt are one of the challenges you may face. Bringing your emotions to the forefront and confronting them is another.

Your entire belief system may have been altered by an abusive relationship in the past, and it's time to assess what you believe in and why at this point in your journey. The same goes for your thoughts and the way you express yourself through actions and words. Are you defensive? Are you angry? Are you resentful? If so, it's time to literally pick your brain and assess where you stand emotionally and mentally at this part in your journey.

By assessing your thoughts and how you express yourself, it's also easier to determine your current attitude regarding your present and your future. It may take some time to develop the attitude you want, but knowing where you are now and where you want to be in the future can help guide you along the way. The same goes for your actions.

Self-discovery literally helps you find yourself. It defines who you are, and will help guide you to where you want to be. Self-reflection, personality, and your attitudes will determine how you make that journey. You can go through life being angry and resentful, but in the long run, doing so won't help you overcome your past, transform your present, or embrace your future.

We've discussed the importance of reclaiming your emotions and releasing anger, as well as the powerful potential of forgiveness and belief in yourself.

Self-Discovery – the MIA Approach

Follow a few guidelines to help you along your journey to self-discovery and healing. You can do this several ways, including:

- **Make time for yourself** - "Me" time is important in any healing process. You've been in a bad place, and now it's time to regain your footing. This may involve quite a bit of self-reflection. Don't run from it. Rather, embrace it and confront negative emotions in order to get them out in the open so that you can focus on more positive aspects of your future.

- **Contemplation** - Find a peaceful place that you enjoy. It can be at your local park, on a hillside, or during a daily walk. When you're by yourself, it's time to contemplate your satisfaction, or dissatisfaction, with life. While we encourage everyone to focus on the positive, there are times when we can't ignore the negative, or aspects of our lives that are discouraging. In such cases, it's important to understand why. It's only when we understand *why* something is discouraging that we can take steps to change it.

- **Plan** - Develop a short-term and long-term plan to help you deal with the negatives in your life. The positives are great, and should be pursued, but get rid of the monkey on your back caused by your past by dealing with those situations and emotions as completely as possible. While we don't want you to dwell on such negative emotions, we will say again that it's important to address them. Pushing them into a compartment of your mind and forgetting about them isn't really helpful. While we don't want to relive a bunch of negative experiences in our lives, we can learn something from them, if we allow ourselves to. You've overcome something enormous. Take strength from that. You are a strong person, and can overcome your past. We're not saying that it's going to be easy or simple, but it can be done.

The great philosopher Aristotle once said, "*Knowing yourself is the beginning of all wisdom.*" There's something to be said about that. You can't be afraid to look at yourself in the mirror, and you can't be afraid to change things. It's natural to operate within our comfort zones, but sometimes, it's beneficial to venture beyond those comfort zones and experience something different in life.

Chinese philosopher Lao Tzu once said, "*At the center of your being you have the answer; you know who you are and you know what you want.*"

Digging deep beneath the surface is an important aspect of your journey toward self-discovery. "*Until you make the unconscious conscious, it will direct your life and you will call it fate,*" said C. G. Jung, and that is also very true.

Conclusion

Find someone who inspires you and look around you every day. You're likely to find inspiration in the simplest things in life. Your journey toward self-discovery is something that can happen every day, without you being consciously aware of it.

Take the time to get to know yourself again. Overcoming

an abusive or violent past is challenging and difficult, but you've already taken the first step. Continue on your journey toward self-discovery, and focus on healing. In the next section, we'll offer you some steps you can take toward emotional healing that will help you overcome your past, transform your present, and enable you to embrace your future with open arms.

Chapter 5

Beginning to Heal –Keys to Emotional Healing

Though it may take some time, wounds on our body eventually heal. We may bear the scars for a while, but we do heal. Emotional healing is not seen, but is an important aspect for overall health and wellness.

Emotional healings assures your ability to exist in the here and now and overcome the scars from your past. Many people will offer you suggestions on how you can begin to heal emotionally, and many of those ideas are very good, while others may not suit you. However, do give them all a chance, whether a friend, a counselor, your pastor, or a family member offers them. There is no one right way or wrong way to begin healing – it's a process that begins inside, in our heart.

Many of us overcoming a violent or abusive past struggle with not only the physical ramifications, but also the emotional damage caused by such a history. Many of us pretend that it never existed and literally sweep them under a rug, or package them into a nice neat box in our memory and pretend they're not there. Others hang onto it, unable to get past the memories.

However, emotional healing is not only vital for our
spiritual well-being, but our overall mental and emotional
health, both short-term and long-term. In this section, we'll
introduce a number of methods, (call them what you will;
keys, steps, tips) that will help you start your journey
toward emotional health and wellness.

Emotional Healing – the MIA Approach

Key #1: Face the facts. The truth of the matter is, you were
involved in a violent or domestically abusive relationship.
You can't pretend that it didn't happen, and living in denial
only promotes negative emotions that may very well
manifest in physical symptoms.

Many of us are certainly quite adept at building protective
barriers around ourselves, and once we're out of such a
relationship, we would like nothing more than forget about
it and shove it in the past. However, acting as if nothing
happened or nothing is wrong is damaging.

Key#2: Confess your own faults or shortcomings. We all
make mistakes, and nobody expects you to be perfect.
Share your feelings and emotions regarding your decision
to even get involved in your past relationship with someone
you trusted. Yes, it was a mistake, and it ended badly, but
it's important to look in the mirror and ask yourself a
number of questions.

Key #3: Take responsibility. Yes, if someone physically or emotionally, mentally, sexually or in any other way abused you, that is their fault. However, it's important to accept your own personal responsibility with the situation. You'll never free yourself from the past unless you're willing to admit that, in some way, you also share some personal responsibility for your past. You met the person, you moved in with him, things like that. Did you deliberately marry or get involved with a drug addict, an alcoholic, or someone you knew might not be the ideal person for you, and yet you ignored your gut instincts and did it anyway?

We're certainly *not* attempting to blame you for the domestic or violent abuse, but we all make decisions in life. Some of them are good and some of them don't turn out too well. This is what we're talking about; those poor decisions you've made, or the decisions you made that you thought were good and that turned out bad. Then, ask yourself what happened. Did you go into a relationship with blinders on? Did you go into a relationship knowing that that person wasn't exactly an ideal partner, but thought that perhaps, you could change him?

Yes, something was done to us against our will. However, did we allow that situation to grow? Did we allow it to persist? Did we hesitate to take control over our own lives and get out of that relationship? We certainly understand that many women trapped in such relationships feel as if they have a very few options to escape. We've been there.

This exercise is not meant to point fingers of blame on an abused individual, as often, abuse is well beyond their control. However, it's also important to recognize that our decisions and actions often put us into situations that are difficult to get out of. By engaging in such self-reflection, we can, hopefully, learn from our errors in judgment so that we never find ourselves in such a position again.

Here's another way of looking at it, from a spiritual perspective:

First: Acknowledge that we need to heal. In order for us to receive healing, we must first admit that we are hurting.

Second: Find the source of the pain. It's easy to identify and define pain that we feel on our body, but emotional pain is a little more difficult to pinpoint. Emotionally, what exactly causes you pain? Is it that you weren't respected, you weren't appreciated, or that you were made to feel less than worthy? Find that pain, and acknowledge it. It's at that point in time that your faith may offer the greatest balm.

Third: Clean yourself of emotional wounds. How do you clean yourself of an emotional wound? Recognize, address and deal with anger, depression, and bitterness. Forgive. Negative emotions are more than harmful to our emotions and spirit than many realize, and may eventually contribute to physical symptoms. Many of us are able to rely heavily on our faith in God or our religion to forgive and cleanse us.

Most importantly, you must be willing and ready to receive and accept healing. Many of us want to hang onto our anger, our grief, and our bitterness, but such emotions are not conducive to the emotional healings that enables us to move on. We mentioned before that an ability to forgive offers a great burst of freedom to those who do so. While forgiveness can be beneficial, it is only effective when we are open to receiving the healing benefits of such forgiveness.

Gather your strength. Those of us who are emotionally damaged need to strengthen our spirits and courage. We want to take steps to make sure that nothing like this ever happens to us again. Therefore, we need to gain strength, physically, emotionally, and mentally. Even if we've been emotionally bruised and battered, we need to focus on strengthening our minds, our spirit, and our attitudes. In such a way, we can literally overcome the physical and emotional damages of the past.

A Three-Step Approach to Dealing with Your Pain

As we mentioned before, there is no one right way or wrong way to begin emotionally healing from an abusive or violent past. Some of us can accomplish amazing things if we just allow ourselves to get into touch with how we feel. Most of us don't like remembering bad things, but emotional pain can severely inhibit and restrict your ability to move on in life. Suppressing, repressing, and denying an emotional pain may make you appear stronger on the outside, but only suffices in weakening your spirit and your resistance.

Try the following steps to deal with your pain:

Step one - Get familiar with your pain. Identify it and accept it.

Step two - Deal with it. How? Crying is one of the most emotionally beneficial methods of dealing with emotional pain. Many of us refuse to cry as we think crying conveys weakness. However, crying is a very basic human emotion that allows us to release emotional pain. Crying isn't the only expression of emotional pain, but if you have to, scream, yell, growl or snarl into your pillow. Pound on your pillow or a soft object, (or anything that won't hurt you).

Crying and intense physical activity is an excellent method of releasing tension, emotional hurt, anger, and frustration. It's cleansing. It doesn't matter whether you cry for five minutes or five hours; the important thing is that you're breaking through the barrier that you've built and allowed feelings to take over. Therefore, even through crying, you gain control.

Step three - Assess. After you've cried (and some people literally exhaust themselves through crying or release of intense emotion), sit down and assess how you feel.

Reevaluate your thought processes, your perceptions, and your emotions. In many cases, after release and resulting relief of intense emotion, you'll find that your mind and body is prepared to deal with new emotions or changes. The mind has released some of its pain and is ready to move on.

It's important to remember that your mind is truly powerful. Forcing your way past emotional pain means leaving a part of yourself behind, and introducing certain aspects of the new you to the person looking in the mirror. You may not be done with crying just yet. For some, this process toward self-healing takes days or weeks, and sometimes, months.

Releasing Emotions

The bottom line is to let your emotions out. Whatever step you take toward emotional healing, it's important to do it at your own pace. The emotions involved in overcoming a violent or abusive relationship are often associated with the grieving process. It's as powerful and numbing as grieving the death of a loved one. Most of the stages of overcoming an abusive relationship are likened to the stages of overcoming grief. The stages of grief and mourning are defined as:

- Denial
- Anger
- Bargaining

- Depression
- Acceptance

Yes, you'll ride quite an emotional roller coaster, but in the end, your body, mind, and spirit will be cleansed through your ordeal. We're not telling you that you'll forget, or that some aspects of your past won't carry on into the future. They're your experiences, and they are what have shaped you to be the person you are today. However, it's important to realize that emotional healing is truly one of the most important aspects of overcoming one's past and being able to move forward.

Our next section will focus on overcoming your past. By utilizing all the suggestions offered so far, you'll be amazed at your ability to look forward, rather than backward.

Chapter 6

Overcoming Your Past

It's easy for some people to say "get over it,", but there's much more involved in overcoming your past than sweeping it under a rug, pretending it never happened, or thinking that you can get over it in a day or two. Overcoming your past is an extensive journey of self-discovery, and depending on individuals, may take months or even years.

Every one of us would go about overcoming our past in a different way, depending on our circumstances, our personality, and our emotional stability. Overcoming violence and abuse is never easy, especially in a domestic relationship. You're not dealing with stranger abuse, but abuse from someone you loved, whether it's a parent, a child, or a spouse.

The problem is that if you don't move forward, you may become mired in your past. By doing nothing, you accomplish nothing. That sounds harsh, but it's true. For example, after you've left a violent or abusive past behind you, it may be difficult to trust again. Finding new love, companionship, and loyalty can seem an insurmountable challenge. That's because your situation was scary, and it's natural to feel wary or suspicious of relationships in the future.

In many ways, your emotions, especially any feelings of love, are tied to negative emotions. Our memories help shape our present. However, we have to face our bad feelings or emotions in order to grow, move forward, and transform our lives from the negative to the positive. Avoiding relationships is a natural inclination, but isn't necessarily healthy.

If you feel you need some help digging into such emotions, we would suggest a visit with your pastor, a close and trusted friend, or a counselor or therapist. Remember however, that there is a difference between recognizing those negative feelings and 'letting go' of those negative feelings.

It's also important not to let past experiences define who you are or serve as the foundation for decisions you make in the future. It may sound trite right now, but just because you had one or two bad relationships doesn't mean the next one will be bad. Just because you had a horrible experience doesn't mean that your life is worthless, or that you'll never get where you want to be.

It may feel - right now - like you can't get over these negative feelings, self-doubt, or lack of self-confidence, but rest assured, you can. Lean on your faith. Lean on your friends and family.

MIA Approach

Taking the First Step

There is no right way or wrong way to overcome your past. However, there may be some questions that you can ask yourself that will help you begin to understand where you've been as well as where you want to go. We all have regrets, no doubt about it. However, with regret comes growth, knowledge, enlightenment, and understanding. No, we don't want to make the same mistakes, but we also have to accept the fact that we are human, and mistakes will likely occur in our future. However, the key is not to let the fear of such mistakes hamper your efforts to grow.

For example, many women coming out of a violent or abusive relationship may ask herself where she went wrong. After all, in most cases, you loved this person. You trusted him. Whether the abuse and violence happened overnight or took years to develop, it's not easy to admit that you might've misjudged someone. Of course, this is a whole other issue. It's impossible to really get to know someone until you live with them day in and day out. Chances are, if we knew someone was violent or abusive, we wouldn't willingly put ourselves in such a situation.

However, it's important for us to be responsible for our decisions as well as the consequences. Don't kick yourself for making a bad decision, or for having held out hope that your loved one would change, or for believing that you

could change your spouse, your parent, or your adult child
from their violent or abusive ways.

Forgive Yourself

The first step toward overcoming your past is to forgive
yourself for making mistakes. We've talked about this
before, but we're mentioning it again because it is so
important. Without forgiveness, you'll live a life of
resentment, anger, and dissatisfaction. Don't condemn
yourself forever for mistakes. Yes, you have overcome a
horrible situation, but now it's time to look forward and
start fresh. Many of us learn our lessons the hard way, and
we're not saying this lightly.

Find Friendship

Regardless of your circumstances, you know who your true
friends are by this time. Identify these individuals as well
as family members or relatives that have stood by you that
continue to want to offer you support. Don't be ashamed or
embarrassed to accept their help. We all need a helping
hand once in a while, and often, overcoming our past
means learning to trust and rely on others again.

Recognize Your Difference

You are different individual now than you were then. Just

the fact that you've left a violent or abusive relationship should prove that to you. Yes, you may feel a little jaded, critical, or suspicious of everyone and anything, but deep down, you can be proud of yourself for leaving an abusive relationship. The uncertainties of our future make such a decision extremely difficult for many.

Persevere

Now is not the time to give up. We all experience bad days and we all throw ourselves little pity parties, but try not to mope too long. Give yourself a chance to grieve, and to feel sorry for yourself, but then it's time to dust yourself off, get back on your feet, and start looking forward again. Yes, you may have been knocked to your knees, but now it's time to stand up for yourself and experience a new start. Accept the mistakes and the regrets and then look forward. Learn from those mistakes and regrets to make your life more fulfilling in the future.

Conclusion

We understand that overcoming your past is not an overnight journey, and may take years. In the meantime, focus also on your present and your future. You are responsible for yourself. Rely on your faith, your friends, and your family to help you through this transition from past to present. Our next section will offer several tips and strategies to help you exist in the now, and transform your present, putting you in a good position to not only overcome your past, but to embrace your future.

Chapter 7

Transforming Your Present

How do you go about transforming your present? Many of us say we *want* to change, but don't quite know how to go about it. In its most simplistic terms, transforming your present requires careful thought and understanding of where you've been, and a firm decision to change your attitude, your way of thinking, and even your mental outlook on life.

Basically, ask yourself this: ***What do I want to do for the rest of my life?***

Motivational speakers are great at lighting a fire under us, but it's up to us to follow through. In some ways, transforming your present is a gigantic leap of faith. Many of us have an affirmed, deep belief in God and in our faith, and therefore, initiating such a change in our environment may not be quite as challenging or scary as it is for others. However, it's lack of faith, whether we're talking about faith in God, or of faith in ourselves or in overcoming challenges, that prevents many of us from not only overcoming our past, but in our inability to transform our present.

Mohammed Ali, one of the world's greatest boxers once

said, "*It's lack of faith that makes people afraid of meeting challenges, and I believed in myself.*"

Creating a Vision

Imagine yourself in your future. What do you want to see? Don't let negative self-talk or negative feelings and emotions prevent you from reaching your fullest potential. Self- doubt is a literal enemy of many of us, an aspect of our development that prevents us from making our dreams come true or succeeding in life.

Of course, we all experience doubts and uncertainties in life. It's natural. After all, we're human. However, if we don't take that leap, or even try, where do we end up? So what if you fail? Learn from it. Gain experience from it . It's natural to want to succeed in everything we do, but transforming your present doesn't happen overnight, just as overcoming your past doesn't. However, as you strive to challenge yourself, it's important to also focus on the here and now. Enjoy daily pleasures wherever possible. If you have to actively seek out such pleasure, do so.

Not long ago, we met a woman who had come out of an abusive relationship. She felt despondent, exhausted, and confused. She was middle-aged, divorced, with very limited real work experience, and didn't know how she would support herself. She struggled with depression and thoughts of hopelessness, but one day, she decided to do

something, anything to change her surroundings.
Walking down the street, she began noticing things around
her. She looked up to the mountains, felt the warm sun on
her face, and, for the first time in a long time, realized that
life continued around her, despite her emotional trauma.
She smiled. Then, rounding a corner, she saw the dog
pound. She walked inside, smiling once again at the sound
of yapping dogs, and then noticed a sign asking for
volunteers.

Long story short, this woman made an effort to volunteer at
the dog pound every morning. The faith, companionship,
trust and loyalty that the dogs showed her as she fed them
lightened her spirits. Eventually, she was hired as a part-
time employee, and then, two months later, was asked if
she could go full time. She did.

Today, this woman is the manager of the dog pound, and is
an active member in her community when it comes to
rescuing animals from abusive homes or dangerous
situations.

Why are we sharing that story? Because we want to
illustrate that you never know what's around the corner.
Different things make us happy. Find the things that bring a
smile to your lips and help you feel energized and more
confident in yourself.

Creating a Vision – the MIA Approach

Try this exercise: Create a written statement that clearly and specifically defines how you want to grow in certain areas of your life. Do this for:

- Personal growth
- Spiritual growth
- Relationships
- Career
- Finances
- Health and fitness

Be as specific as you can, envisioning yourself next week, next month, or next year. When you imagine yourself in these aspects in your future, you're more likely to achieve success.

Who Am I?

Most importantly, be yourself! When striving to transform your present, it's important to remember who you are. Be yourself. Self-improvement doesn't require that you turn into a stranger. You don't have to look or act like anyone else, because you're you. You're wonderful just the way you are. Take the time to sit with yourself, explore your soul, your psyche, and your impact on those around you. Most importantly, embrace who you are and take pride in your abilities. Recognize your weaknesses, and always strive for self-improvement.

When striving for transformation in your present, it's also important to expect the best from yourself. Remember that in order to get something, you usually have to give something. Give away those negative feelings. Toss away those inklings of self-doubt and low self-esteem. Expect the best from yourself and your dreams. Sure, we might have to take a few detours along the way to where we're going, but sooner or later, we'll get there. Don't be a victim.

You are worthwhile. You are valuable. Imagine yourself in positive situations with pleasant and happy scenarios. Bottom line, expect the best.

Many of us ask ourselves, before we make any decision or doing something, what's the worst that can happen? In some cases, that's an important question, especially if it surrounds your safety or that of anyone else around you. However, when seeking to transform your present, it's also important to imagine the best thing or best outcome that can happen.

Every decision requires assessment of pros and cons. You may be a glass half-empty type of person, but try to switch your outlook from the glass is half empty to the glass is half full type of mindset. Caution is a good thing, but at times, it may also hold us back.

Conclusion

Like overcoming your past, transforming your present requires your active participation. When you change yourself in the here and now, you're preparing yourself for the future. No one knows what the future will bring, but it's important to keep looking forward rather than backward. In our next section, we'll talk about this in a little more detail.

Chapter 8

Embracing Your Future

The future can be scary. No one knows what's going to happen tomorrow, next week, or next year, let alone five or ten years down the line. Besides that, what exactly does it mean to embrace your future? It can mean many different things to many different people.

Embracing your future may involve going to school or in some way improving your educational level so that you can attain the goals you set for yourself. Embracing your future may also focus on implementing steps to help you improve your sense of self-esteem and confidence. However, embracing your future incorporates more than career development and self-help programs that improve you as a person.

It's All about Attitude

Embracing your future also incorporates your mental and emotional attitudes about life now, and what life can be in the future. In order to better your future and your chances of getting where you want to be, it's important to know what you're looking for. That's not always an easy question to answer. We all want security. We all want to feel as if our contributions are important, not only to our families, but to those around us, whether that's at work, school, or within a community.

Your future is a powerful incentive in overcoming your past. Where you're going is more important than where you've been, although for many of us, our past controls our every move and decision toward that future. However, it's time to get rid of the shame, the sacrificing, the judgment and guilt you may feel about your past. Instead, you need to surround yourself with positive emotions and thoughts, friends, and supporters.

The most important part when planning for your future is to determine where you want to get. For example, what single action or decision can you make right this minute that will help you embrace your future plans and aspirations?

Envision yourself in your future. In the last section, you wrote down your vision statements. These visions will help you attain your goals and remind you on a daily basis what you're working so hard to attain. Setting goals is action-based. Stay proactive rather than waiting for life to happen to you. We can't always control everything going on around us, but you can control yourself and your own decisions.

While we don't always make the right decisions, making a decision is an important first step in embracing your future. When you look back from yesterday, or even today to a future moment, you are in control. We're not suggesting that by merely imagining something that you can attain it, but that your vision can help set you along the right path. When embracing your future, you need to take a few steps. These steps may seem simplistic, but they're not. Take a look and employ the **MIA Approach:**

Decide what you want - that seems like quite a simple statement doesn't it? However, you need to know what you want, or where you want to be, in order to start your journey toward that goal. We asked you to be as specific as you can when writing down what you're looking for or what you want. A vision or daydream that incorporates your goal isn't enough, because we can't wait for life to miraculously give us what we're looking for. You need to work for it.

After you've written down your list of things that you want or would like to accomplish in life, pick the first one that you honestly believe, that right now, you can attain or accomplish, with some effort, of course. For now, focus on that one thing and put the rest aside.

As you work toward one goal at the time, it's important to focus. We can all dream or aspire to achieve dozens, if not hundreds of things, but for now, let's just stick with one. Remember that old quote, "*The journey of one thousand miles begins with a single step.*"

Focus, focus, focus - it's important to apply adequate attention, focus as well as energy to attain the goal you've set for yourself. This goal may be short-term, to be achieved in a week or two, while other goals are set farther into the future. As you work on reaching the first goal you set for yourself, you'll find that action has a way of a lightening the spirits and creating a sense of excitement.

Provide yourself with a positive focus on this first goal that you want to attain on a daily basis before you go to sleep and when you wake up in the morning. Imagine that you have successfully reached this first goal, and imagine how you'll feel when you do. With these thoughts in mind, your subconscious attitudes change, and you'll find your confidence and self-esteem growing.

Action - after you've chosen a goal, it's time to act. The past is the past and needs to stay there. Now it's time to focus on the action or actions you need to begin your journey toward attaining your first goal. Start with small steps, and as your self-confidence and self-esteem grows, you'll find yourself taking bigger steps. Keep putting one foot ahead of the other, deal with daily struggles and responsibilities, but always, always keep your ultimate goal in mind.

Don't give up - there may be times when you feel your goal is unattainable, especially if you run into a lot of obstacles along the way. Be conscientious about choosing an attainable goal, but if you do find one that is too challenging to deal with right now, put it aside and choose another one that may be easier to accomplish.

We're not suggesting you change your mind at the first obstacle, but use common sense and set your goals as realistically as possible. For example, let's say you want to earn a college degree. However, between work obligations and scheduling, you may not be able to obtain the classes you're looking for, or you may not be able to receive the funding assistance that you require. Instead of letting this derail you, find a way to get around the obstacle. You may need to focus on your employment for a while, and then give a college another try.

Some goals are easier to achieve than others, but the bottom line is to never give up or quit on your goals until they are accomplished. You may need to switch things up once in awhile or take detours, but the important thing is to keep moving forward. This is the basic concept of someone embracing his or her future. Your future isn't going to fall in your lap. You need to go after it. First however, you need to identify what you're looking for.

Conclusion

Overcoming your past, transforming your present, and embracing your future takes careful thought and consideration. However, one of the most common things that prevents people from reaching their goals is... not family, not friends, and not your past. It's you.

You must have the grit and determination to get where you

want to be. All of us have to work hard for what we want in life. Often, it's a daily struggle. However, it's not just going to happen because we wish it so. Sure, we all want to be millionaires, but few of us ever will be. Does that stop us from dreaming big? In most cases, no. After all, the journey there may offer us a number of challenges and rewards that help us become better human beings.

Take the time to determine what you want. The journey toward your goals is not always an easy one, and your goals may change as you travel along the road leading into your future. Still, it's the journey that counts. To make that journey, you need to understand yourself and how you feel about yourself. We'll talk about this a little more in the next section.

Chapter 9

Understanding Yourself and the Power of Self Love

This section is all about you. It's about learning how to understand yourself as well as encompassing the far-reaching power of self-love. How do you understand yourself? That may seem simple to many people, but it actually requires some reflection. It requires you to be brutally honest - something that many people are not willing to do.

For the purposes of this section, we'd like to ask you to go stand in front of a mirror. Look at yourself. What do you see? What do you think other people see when they look to you? Is your opinion of yourself different from how others may think of you?

When we talk about self-love, we're not talking about being conceited or arrogant. We're talking about accepting who you are and then taking steps to change some of the less-than-stellar aspects of your personality or your attitude.

When it comes to understanding yourself, you have to know how you feel about yourself and others around you. You don't need to be an egomaniac or egocentric to experience self-love. Self-love, at its most basic definition, can be defined as someone who respects herself, takes responsibility for her actions, and cares about herself. Again, it's important to be honest about your strengths as well as your weaknesses. We all have weaknesses. It's part of being human. However, it's also important to realize that in order for others to love you, you also have to love yourself.

Again, we'd like to emphasize that this concept of self-love is not at all arrogant or conceited in nature. When we speak of self-love, we're talking about self-image, self-esteem, and self-awareness. Often, when we're unhappy with our circumstances or with our life, it's because we feel inadequate, or that we have been wronged, or even that we have made mistakes from which we can never recover. These are self-defeating thoughts that compel many of us to remain stuck in place.

Let's get back to the mirror. When you look in the mirror, are you looking at only your body's surface, or deeper inside? A person who is confident and self-assured recognizes flaws in skin or appearance, but doesn't let that bother them. Others absolutely hate looking in the mirror because they see every freckle, skin blemish, the wrong color eyes, or the wrong shape of the nose or chin. Such individuals tend to not only feel unhappy about their appearance on the outside, but themselves on the inside because, again, they feel as if they're not quite up to par with everyone else.

What, exactly is self-love then? Self-love is not expressed just in the things that we do or say, but who we are as a person. If you fake emotions all day long, you're not being true to yourself. Self-love also requires that you see yourself as a valuable individual, whether you live by yourself or in a huge family. Every person on earth has the ability to contribute to human kind and nothing can change that.

When you care about yourself, you can care about others. You don't like seeing other people or animals mistreated. A person who understands herself and the power of self-love understands and realizes that mistakes can be made, but that it's important to learn from those mistakes rather than disparaging herself over them.

A person who understands herself is also able to experience the joys in life, even when trying new and often challenging things. A person who loves herself takes responsibility for mistakes, and doesn't allow herself to feel guilty over it for months or even years. They don't make excuses, to anyone else or themselves. They admit a mistake or error in judgment, accept it, and move on.

How do you love yourself? Let's start with these using the **MIA Approach:**

- Don't berate yourself. Self-criticism is not constructive. When we make a mistake, we can learn from it, and take steps not to repeat it.

- Learn to love yourself - how do you do that? Accept your strengths and your weaknesses or flaws. Humans are imperfect, but that doesn't mean that you're not worthy or valuable. Be kind to yourself and the next time you look in the mirror, smile at your reflection and look beneath the surface to find yourself.

- Live kindness - be kind and considerate and gentle of others. You'll feel better. When you're kind to others, you'll feel good about yourself. This positive emotion empowers and supports your growth and development.

- It's the thought that counts - acknowledge your efforts, even if you come up short sometimes. When you do your best, you know that you have given it your all, even if your efforts failed to produce the results you're looking for.

- Quit worrying all the time - yes, we constantly worry about finances, our careers, and how we're going to accomplish things. However, instead of just worrying about it, take steps to address those worries. Being proactive is better than wallowing in self-pity and helps you take steps to change your current situation.

- Trust - trust yourself. Sure, you've made mistakes in the past, and right now, you might be feeling pretty low, unworthy, and a burden to others around you. However, this is the ideal time to make changes. We talked earlier about creating goals and visualizing outcomes. Do that.

- Be honest - be honest about your feelings. Whether you're happy or sad, acknowledge those feelings. Don't fool or lie to yourself and think that you can succeed in burying your emotions. Get them out. Whether you write them down, cry into a pillow, or talk to God, get your emotions out. Holding them inside can eventually lead to emotional as well as physical damage to your body.

- Be ready to forgive - be ready to forgive yourself for making past mistakes. We all make mistakes, and will continue to do so in the future. Don't beat yourself up over it, because they're in the past. Acknowledge them, accept them, and learn from them.

- Be grateful - you may think you don't have anything to be grateful for, but you do. Be grateful for your strengths, aptitudes, skills, and the very fact that you're alive and are now stepping forward on a journey to make differences in your life. Appreciate the little things around you; a rising sun, a happy puppy, the smile of a child.

- Work on your self-confidence - actively seek out situations that will help you build your sense of confidence and self-esteem. If you have a particular skill or aptitude, find ways to use it, in your family life, or in your community.

- Find some fun - we often get too serious in our lives. What did you like to do when you were a child? Have you done it recently? Find something that you have fun doing and then do it. Bring daily joy into your life by taking time for yourself.

- Take care of yourself - when we're vulnerable, we tend to let ourselves go. Many of us turn to comfort eating or self-destructive behaviors such as drinking or drugs. Instead, treat your body like the temple and force yourself to get enough to eat and enjoy daily exercise. Exercise releases endorphins; your body's own "feel good" hormones that will help lift your mood.

- Look around - every day, go outside and find something beautiful. It doesn't matter whether it's a cherry tree in full bloom, the Mallard duck floating in the neighborhood pond, or a sunset over the mountains or the ocean. Learn to seek the beauty around you every day, and you'll realize that there are still plenty of things that you can smile and be happy about.

Conclusion

Many of us overcoming a violent or abusive relationship have taken the first step in getting out of that relationship, but then what? The next section will provide a list of helpful resources and support systems that you may rely on in times of need. Then, we'll move on to help you learn how to identify what a healthy relationship is and how to overcome your fear to love again.

Chapter 10

Helpful Resources and Support Systems

You're never completely alone. Resources for abused women are out there. While getting out of an abusive relationship is one of the hardest things you'll ever do, it's just the beginning of your journey. Next comes healing. Find help for that. You don't have to go it alone.

Below, we've listed several options, resources and support systems to help you take those steps toward recovery and self-reliance.

AARDVARC - a national Abuse, Rape, and Domestic Violence Aid and Resource is a non-profit resource founded in 1996, receiving its non-profit status in 2001. It's created by victims themselves, striving to help others by providing support, guidance, and most importantly, empathy. They've been there. They know what you're feeling.

http://www.aardvarc.org/victim/states/

The **Domestic Violence Resource Center** in Oregon
provides a number of support and services, from counseling
to outreach, to shelters and more. They offer services such
as protective order advocacy programs, a 24-hour crisis
line, and numerous community outreach programs. They're
located in Oregon, serving Washington, Clackamas and
Multnomah counties, but their downloadable brochures,
resource card and flyers provide advice and guidance.

Website: http://dvrc-or.org/

Brochure: http://dvrc-
or.org/images/uploads/39305_DVRC_ENGLISH_trifold_b
rochure.pdf?phpMyAdmin=3e2639ceb8ed94505c331c7bc3
c8d871

Resource Card: http://dvrc-
or.org/images/uploads/39304_DVRC_ENGLISH_four_pan
el_resource_card.pdf?phpMyAdmin=3e2639ceb8ed94505c
331c7bc3c8d871

**Office for Victims of Crime – Domestic and Family
Violence**: http://ovc.ncjrs.gov/topic.aspx?topicid=27

The Office of Justice Programs is a government-sponsored
national resource program that offers numerous resources

for victims of crime.

Access the link below to find over 60 resources funded by the Office for Victims of Crimes.

http://ovc.ncjrs.gov/topic.aspx?topicid=27

National Domestic Violence Hotline:
http://www.thehotline.org/resources/

Here you'll find a number of links and resource materials to help you be safe and to offer support.

Or call 1.800.799.7233 or for TTY call 1.800.787.3224

Helpguide.org:

http://www.helpguide.org/mental/domestic_violence_abuse_help_treatment_prevention.htm

Provides invaluable information on abused and battered women in regard to safety, planning, shelters and restraining orders and more.

Womenslaw.org :

http://www.womenslaw.org/gethelp_type.php?type_name=State%20and%20Local%20Programs

Offers a state-by-state directory of shelters for those
escaping from domestic violence. The site also offers
resources for local programs in your community or region,
information on finding a lawyer, local Sheriff's
departments and courthouse locations, as well as national
organizations, chat and message boards.

Chapter 11

How to Identify Healthy Relationships

It stands to reason, especially when you're recovering from an abusive or domestically abusive relationship, that you might feel hesitant to even think of entering a new relationship. However, take some steps to help you identify whether your relationships are apt to be healthy rather than detrimental and traumatic.

We'll mention a few of them in this section, but it's important to remember that there are never any guarantees in life. We all think differently, look at things differently, and have different instincts, depending on our upbringing, our culture, and our expectations.

What is a healthy relationship?

What exactly constitutes a healthy relationship? Here are a few questions to help you identify whether past or present relationships are healthy, and questions that you can ask yourself before entering into a deeper relationship with someone.

For Example:

- Do you take the responsibility for finding happiness

for yourself or do you expect someone else to make you happy? Sure, we're all seeking happiness from our partners, but it's not their responsibility to make us happy. Happiness comes from inside.

- Do you or your partner keep your word? If you or he says that something will be done, is it done? Keeping your word builds trust in someone else, and vice versa. If you find that a new partner or friend is not keeping his word, and consistently doesn't keep their promises, that may be a red flag that something in the relationship (friendship, romantic, parental, etc.) is not healthy and needs to be assessed.

- Are you able to admit mistakes? Is your partner? The ability to admit when a mistake is made is a sign of a healthy mental attitude. Blaming everyone else but yourself for your mistakes, or someone who does so, lacks honesty, responsibility, and trust. We've seen this repeatedly with narcissistic behavioral types - people who consistently blame others for their shortcomings or failures in life.

- Do you attempt to resolve problems or issues? Hiding problems under the rug or refusing to acknowledge and address them are not signs of a healthy relationship. Do you expect a partner to be perfect? If you do, your relationship may be doomed for failure, because no one is perfect. At the same time, it's important to acknowledge that all relationships have their ups and downs, disagreements, and conflicts. A successful and healthy long-term relationship relies on your and your partner's ability to discuss issues honestly and openly. After all, we don't agree with others all the time, and you can't expect to do that in a relationship.

- If you ask yourself whether you'd be better off outside of the relationship than inside it, chances are it's time to assess your situation. If you ask yourself this question and your answer is "no", then chances are you are in a healthy relationship, even though you're experiencing some ups and downs.

- Do you listen to your partner? Listening is a skill, and sometimes, we have to develop that skill in order to truly hear and understand what someone else is saying. When you're willing to listen to your partner, you're engaging in healthy communication, which in turn, enhances a healthy relationship.

- Do you constantly hide things from your partner? Whether it's your feelings, your opinion, or money, hiding things from your partner is not a sign of a healthy, open relationship. It's important to discuss your feelings, good or bad, in a relationship, and approach difficulties without feeling judged or judging in return.

- Are you clingy? Do you give your partner space, and does he give you space in return? Overly jealous, domineering, and suspicious partners do not make for a healthy relationship. In the beginning, you may feel as if he is behaving in such a manner because he cares about you and wants to keep you safe, and this is difficult for many individuals, especially after overcoming an abusive relationship. It's one thing to be protective and cautious, and yet another to be overbearing about it.

These are just a few simple, yet common-sense questions you can ask yourself regarding your relationship. Yes, it's difficult to even consider beginning a new relationship after you've experienced a bad one, but as time goes by, you may find that your attitudes, opinions, and sense of self have changed. Just because one relationship was bad doesn't mean they all are.

However, it's impossible for such an individual not to be extremely cautious and sometimes even wary when developing relationships with others. The pain and the scars of an abusive or violent relationship are still healing, and it's important not to rush things too quickly. However, do open your heart to other options, take things slow, and carefully assess what's going on around you when it comes to any new relationship.

Conclusion

We've mentioned many times how difficult it may be for a person who has overcome an abusive or violent past to feel comfortable sharing, laughing, or even loving again. In the next section, we'll offer some tips on how you can overcome your fear to love again. Then, we'll follow up with some daily affirmations that will help you develop a greater sense of self, identity, and confidence as you move forward to meet your future.

Chapter 12

Overcoming Your Fear to Love Again

As we've mentioned before, it's natural to feel hesitant to love again, especially if you've dealt with a violent past or domestic abuse situation. However, it's psychologically healthy to feel affection, compassion, and closeness with others.

One of the first steps toward overcoming your fear to love again is to determine why you're afraid. We're not just talking about physical abuse here, but your emotional state and your future emotional health and wellness.

"The greatest mistake you can make in life is to continually be afraid you will make one."
Elbert Hubbard

We understand that the most common reasons that you may not feel prepared to love again include but are not limited to fear of:

- Entrapment
- Disapproval of others
- Another commitment
- Being emotionally consumed
- Loss

- Emotional scars that will prevent a healthy
  relationship

Many of us overcome hesitance or fear in our everyday
lives, whether it's starting a new job, going in for an
interview, moving, or ending or beginning a new
relationship. Life is scary. However, if we allow fear to
consume our emotions and actions, we never grow.

It's hard to put yourself out there again. We're afraid of
getting hurt - again. Psychology experts and statistics of
studies have suggested that right this minute, approximately
250,000 inhabitants of the United States alone are afraid of
falling in love.

That's a lot of people avoiding human companionship.
However, victims who have overcome violence and
domestically abusive relationships have a good reason to
drag their feet when it comes to the commitment, the
opening up, and the trusting involved in a loving
relationship. Many who have overcome that failed
relationship are extremely hesitant to enter anything that
might involve even more drama. Miserable relationships
have the ability to scar someone for life, if they allow it.

Most simplistically, a failed relationship occurs because it's
not the right relationship for you or your partner. However,
we can't stress enough how important it is to learn from a
bad relationship in order to prevent further trauma in the
future.

In an effort to overcome your fear of not only loving someone else, but even getting close to someone else, it's important to start slowly and gradually. You don't have to jump into the dating game right away. Meet new people and eventually, you'll find someone who you're interested in getting to know a little better.

Don't expect your fear or hesitance to disappear overnight. Over a period of time, and especially if you take proactive measures, you'll be able to reduce that fear. Gradually, you'll be able to trust again.

To help you get started up on the way, we've offered a few suggestions:

- Recognize the fact that in opening your heart to love, you may end up getting hurt, but you know the old saying, "*Better to have loved and lost than never to have loved at all.*" Find someone who can help you forget your fears, and keep moving forward until you find "the one" – but only if you want that.

- In many cases, you may be afraid because you're not quite ready, emotionally or mentally, to let go of the past. First, it's important to heal yourself, your scars, and your emotional state before you can offer that special someone your true self. Eventually, you'll know when the time is right.

We're not suggesting that you "get over it" because that's

trite and unproductive. To put it more simply, it's important to realize that no matter how often or how badly you've been hurt in the past, you cannot possibly achieve gains in any relationship if you don't risk it. Love involves taking chances, and you'll have to have faith in yourself to know the difference.

Chances are, when you meet someone who you feel drawn to, you'll sense it, deep inside. You won't be afraid, because that person will have a calming, comfortable effect on you. Give it time.

> *"Our greatest glory consists not in never falling, but in rising every time we fall."*
> Oliver Goldsmith

Take it from those who have gone before you, and those who will come after you. You gain strength, confidence, and courage with every experience in your life. An old Japanese saying says that failure teaches success, and it's true. It's not an easy journey, but it is a fulfilling one, if you have the courage to face it.

Overcoming your fear to love again takes time. Don't put unnecessary pressure on yourself to heal at a certain rate. We're all different, and our ability to heal and regain our confidence depends on the type of situations we've been in. Don't compare yourself to others. Just because a friend of yours or family member overcame a bad relationship and then entered another one doesn't mean that you have to.

You'll know when you're ready. When you are, take a deep breath, take that first step, and be aware of how you feel.

When overcoming a bad relationship, or even considering entering a new one, it's important to have the support of friends or family. Find someone who you can open up to, whether that's your best friend or a counselor or psychologist. Bounce your feelings and ideas off others. While you do want to make independent and responsible decisions, it's easy to feel overwhelmed and confused, and the support of friends, family or professional counselors will help you put things in perspective.

Healing and recovery takes time, but someday, rest assured; chances are that you will be ready to love again. We humans crave love, affection, and companionship. How you go about it and at what pace is entirely up to you. Keep your options open, but learn from your lessons or experiences of the past. Don't dwell on them, but do learn from them so that the next time you step forward and enter a relationship, you'll feel better prepared to promote a healthy, loving, and lasting relationship.

Chapter 13

Daily Affirmations

Okay, don't roll your eyes. Every day starting in the morning speak postive life-changing affirmations over your life. Speak a few of your affirmations during the day if you have some private time and before you go to sleep at night. The words we speak help create our world and our experiences. The words we speak are powerful enough to bring in existence what we want out of life. When we speak positive words, we will get positive results and if we speak negative words we get negative results. When you change your words you change your life. Talk the way you want to be and you will become the words you speak. Make your words count. You can approach daily affirmations or positive thinking in any manner that works best for you. There's no one right way or wrong way to go about it. The point of the daily affirmation is to wake up with a singular goal in mind for that day. Whether you're determined to be strong, happy, courageous, or simply want to get through the day without crying, a daily affirmation will help set the tone for your mental and emotional attitude for the day.

Think of it this way: *"Every day I love who I am, transforming my present and embracing my future."*

Starting Over

With every new day comes a new opportunity or a new chance to start over, begin again or renew yourself. Daily affirmations help keep you on track, and are not just effective for those moments when you need the cheerleader section to leap up and give you that boost of confidence.

Daily affirmations, thoughts, or prayers help keep you grounded and focused on what you need to do today - whether it's just for today, or to prepare yourself for tomorrow or next week, these affirmations are an important aspect in finding yourself. Daily affirmations are, at their most basic definition, a conscious thought or prayer that you can say to yourself in the morning when you get up, in the middle of the day when you're feeling stressed, and at night when you go to bed.

An affirmation is typically a short sentence or two that can repeat the same thought or something different every time. Going to the bookstore today, you'll find a number of selections of books that offer daily affirmations for an entire year, but of course, you can also create your own. The idea behind an affirmation or such conscious thoughts is to focus on positive thoughts and images that make you feel better.

Some daily affirmations are faith-based, wherein a reader can access a daily biblical excerpt or phrase. Whether you create your own or purchase a book, or even one that is faith-based, the bottom line is to boost self-esteem, self-confidence, self-acceptance, and self-love.

Do you have to stand in front of a mirror and say, "I love you?" No, but it is suggested that you use a mirror when first starting out with daily affirmations. Why? Because many of us are hesitant to stare at ourselves in the mirror, mostly because we don't want to appear vain. Unfortunately, many of us don't take the time to really look at ourselves. In a private moment, go into the bathroom, close the door, and look at yourself - really look at yourself.

You can use this opportunity to not only explore your exterior, but what's inside. If you feel comfortable, take your daily affirmation or your book of affirmations or prayers into the bathroom with you, and read them while looking in the mirror.

Affirmations are not only for those dealing with alcohol or drug abuse, those struggling through grief, or those seeking greater understanding of their faith, self-confidence, or self-esteem. They're for everyone. They are valuable tools that psychologists recognize today as an effective method of restoring self-confidence and sense of self with clients.

Today, you can find little affirmations on just about everything, from your Starbucks coffee cup to clothing labels and even tea bags, and, of course, fortune cookies. The focus of such statements is to get you to stop and think about yourself for just a moment. While many of us just glance at such affirmations and either smile or agree with them, some of us don't realize the powerful impact they may have on our lives. They're not silly.

For some, daily affirmations help you stay focused on the positive in your life rather than the negative. Taking everything that we've developed in this book and wrapping it up into one nice, neat package will guide you to this point in your life where you look in the mirror and understand who you are, what you want, and the type of future you're looking for.

Affirmations can surround your faith, your career, or your sense (or lack of) self-esteem. For example, say, "I will succeed," in your daily endeavors. The key is to choose affirmations that will help you get through your day, one day at a time. Whether you determine you're not going to cry today, or you're going to help someone to make yourself feel better, just do it.

Affirmations are very powerful mental tools that can help increase your self-confidence and make you feel stronger, calmer, or more prepared to face challenging situations and feelings.

Speaking daily affirmations helps to retrain your thinking by focusing on what you want in life rather than what you do not want. Your brain will begin to believe what you want in life is possible.

Here are some examples of life-changing daily affirmations:

I love and accept my unique self every day

I am a precious gift and I am worthy

I am free to be my best self

I am carrying love and joy in my heart

I am very confident and resilient

I am living the life that I deserve to live

I am whole. I am full of life

I attract only loving and healthy relationships

I am loving, happy, and healthy

I am healed and renewed totally

I know that I deserve love and I accept it every day

I am ready for this new day

I meet each day knowing that good awaits me

The past has no power over my life
I am secure and comforted by the Spirit

I am very blessed and highly favored

I decree and declare something good is going to happen to me today

I decree and declare favor over my life every day

I am free and living with purpose

As I forgive, I am totally set free

I have forgiven others and live totally free

I am prospering in every area of my life

> *"The ancestor of every action is a thought"*
> Ralph Waldo Emerson

Conclusion

In this book, we've covered topics that have hopefully shown you new ways to release your anger and resentment over a violent or abusive past. We've provided a roadmap for you to reclaim your emotions, believe in yourself, and overcome your past so that you can look forward to your future. Our next section will focus on ways to find happiness again. Again, we're not saying that this journey is easy, but it will arrive. You can count on it.

Chapter 14

How to Be Happy Again

Right now, your situation, and even your environment, may seem dismal and hopeless. However, it's important to realize that we all go through highs and lows in our life, and given a chance and an opportunity, most of us manage to crawl out of those valleys and once again attain those mountain tops. The same goes for your emotions. None of us is happy every day. It's impossible. We deal with emotional baggage, the strain of financial obligations, the responsibilities of family.

However, it's important to actively seek happiness. Happiness is around us every day, if we only take the time to look. Yes, happiness is a state of mind, and is not directly related to how much money we have in the bank or our place in society. Sure, a little extra money would make everyone happier, and takes some pressures off of our life, but you know the old saying, "*Money can't buy happiness.*" Money can buy security, but it can't buy happiness.

To find happiness, listen to yourself. Listen to what your body is telling you. Get enough to eat. Try to get enough sleep, and whenever possible, try to exercise every day, whether it's walking around the block or doing a workout in the privacy of your apartment. Make an effort to take care of yourself, inside and out.

What About Me?

Who are you? Are you treating yourself well? Do you find something to do every day that makes you happy, even if it's only for five minutes at a time? Do you enjoy becoming absorbed in a good book? Watching a favorite television show? Do you like watching the sunrise or the sunset? Hiking in the woods, or sitting on a beach?

Do something that makes you happy every day and give it a high priority in your life. While you're engaged in this activity or time of reflection, assess your feelings. Do you feel contentment? Do you feel like you've escaped from the pressures surrounding you, even for five minutes? If you have, you've been successful in creating a moment of happiness.

In order to step with determination along the road to happiness and your future, it's important to reduce the clutter in your life. We're talking about emotional clutter and baggage. Accept what has happened in the past. Whether you're anxious, sad, or afraid, talk to someone about your emotions and feelings. Avoid situations or people that make you sad. We're not talking about avoiding a sick loved one, but avoiding unpleasant people who are negative or critical in nature.

Spend more time talking about things or events that make

you happy rather than things that don't, such as financial difficulties, relationships, or events. We're not saying ignore these things, but try not to dwell on them. Recognize them, acknowledge them, accept them, and then take action to improve your situation.

Most importantly, deal with your problems and find a solution. You may need to try several times, but proactive action has a way of lifting our spirits. When we're doing something about a problem, we feel at least a little more in control of the situation.

Most importantly, when learning to be happy again, it's important to recognize and embrace the happiness around you. Listen to the music you like, or develop a new friendship, and try to find something to do every day that it makes you happy. At the end of the day, right down a least one thing that made you smile or laugh. Such actions create a sense of optimism, curiosity, and even gratitude for your life. Be grateful for what you do have, or the people in your life, or the experiences you've had, rather than dwell only on the negative.

When you feel sad, accept it. We're all allowed to feel sorry for ourselves once in a while. Sadness is as powerful an emotion as laughter, happiness, and joy. Accept the sadness, anxiety, or the fear and then find ways to deal with it. Don't shove it back into the furthest corners of your mind, as this may lead to our inability to move forward. Again, don't beat yourself up for your fears, your grief, or your anxieties. You're human!

If you have to, at least for now, fake happiness. Just like actors take on different roles, you can also pretend to be happy. Even pretending to be happy will, in most cases, make you feel happier. Smiling and laughter reduce stress hormone levels, whether you're faking it or not. Find the joy of spontaneity and be willing, and daring, to try things you normally wouldn't. Volunteer for the local shelter. Offer to babysit for a friend. Take care of someone's pet or adopt one for yourself. Listen to what other people are saying, and share the best of yourself with others.

Conclusion

Be Happy Living the Life You Deserve

Happiness is not something you can physically hold. It comes from within the spirit, the heart, and the mind. Challenge yourself to find contentment, security, and happiness for your life and future. You may need to practice it every day until it becomes a normal part of your existence.

We don't expect you to be happy all the time, as mentioned before, as the daily struggles often leave us worried and unhappy. The important thing is not to let yourself wallow too long. Problems ignored are not problems confronted and dealt with. Even in unpleasant situations and circumstances, proactive action in dealing with problems and obstacles keeps you moving forward rather than static. Focus on being happy again. Practice using those smile muscles in your face, and soon, when you look in the mirror, you find that you're smiling back at yourself.

We hope in this book on overcoming your past, transforming your present, and embracing your future and living the life you deserve has helped you along your way to recovery from a violent or domestic abuse situation.

Overcoming an abusive or violent past or relationship is not easy, but with strength and determination, and a clear view of what you want for your future, you can do it. Rely on your faith. Rely on your friends and loved ones. There is help out there. Never think that you have to go it alone.

You are surrounded by people who love and care about you, whether you realize it or not. Your support system, whether it is faith-based, family-based, or professionally-based, will help you learn how to reclaim your emotions. The power of forgiveness and the ability to believe in yourself will start you on your journey toward self-discovery and healing.

We understand that overcoming your past is not easy, and it doesn't happen overnight. However, with daily determination, you can transform your present existence and begin to make plans for embracing a new future. The most important steps along this journey include an enhanced understanding of yourself and the power that you have over your own emotions, attitudes, and actions.

When moving forward on your journey, it's important to recognize the difference between a healthy and an unhealthy relationship. Pay attention to how you feel about things, and learn from the past. You can be happy again! With determination, you can also overcome your fears to love again. Practice daily affirmations to help you along your way, and you will find yourself growing a little happier and content each day.

You are a precious *Gift* to this world.

Let your light shine !

"Make the most of yourself, for that is all there is of you"
Ralph Waldo Emerson

ABOUT THE AUTHOR

Robert Moment is a life transforming forward-thinking life coach, personal growth strategist, speaker and author.

Robert specializes in maximizing human potential for *happiness*, *purpose* and *success*.

With an ability to take the lessons he's learned in life and apply them to whatever situation someone else is in, Robert Moment excels in bringing out the best in people. His heart and love for people enables him to see who they were meant to be, and then, as a life coach and personal growth strategist, help them to implement a plan to help them reach their goals.

Robert Moment, author of *How Do You Find Happiness, The Path to Emotional Healing and several other life-changing books* , made his mark in the business world working   for some of America's most iconic companies, including Citigroup, Xerox and Sprint-Nextel, among others. He has been described as an innovative trendsetter, with excellent client focus, proficient problem-solving techniques, and extraordinary listening skills, which led him to success as a life coach and personal growth strategist.

Robert Moment doesn't just think *out* of the box, *__he throws the box away!__* Pushing the envelope with innovative ideas that bring out the absolute best in people, his goal is to use his God-given skills to encourage and inspire others to find *and live* their life's purpose.

What can Robert Moment do for you? He can help you transform your adversities into life lessons that will spur you on to the life you are meant to have because he believes that behind every problem is an *opportunity for growth.* While you may not be able to discern what that is, Robert Moment will use his insight and wisdom to best determine what direction you should take.

With years of experience in the corporate sector working for Major Fortune 500 Companies, Robert Moment is now a highly sought-after life coach and personal growth strategist, with the ability to raise people up out of the muck and mire of confusion and doubt into the clear waters of endless possibilities! He recognizes that even the most talented individuals often fail at achieving their goals because they have not yet grasped their life's purpose. Allow him a glimpse into your life and he will use his gifts to reveal to you how to change directions and head toward personal fulfillment and success.

Because Robert Moment believes *everyone* on this earth *has* a purpose, his mission is to help people find it and *live it*. "Experience how good it feels to be happy in life and living your purpose." This is not just a slogan for Robert Moment – *it is a way of life*.

"Be Inspired to Live ™ !"

--- Robert Moment

Visit his website for hope, support and empowerment.

http://www.DomesticAbuseandDomesticViolence.com

Contact Robert for Speaking , Seminar , Workshop and Life Coaching Opportunities:

"Maximizing Human Potential for Purpose, Happiness and Success"

Email:
Robert@DomesticAbuseandDomesticViolence.com

More Information

This book is available for bulk sale. To inquire about pricing for twenty-five copies or more (sold at a substantial discount, non- returnable), please send an email message to:

Robert@DomesticAbuseandDomesticViolence.com

www.ingramcontent.com/pod-product-compliance
Lightning Source LLC
Chambersburg PA
CBHW071013040426
42443CB00007B/753